John E. Phelan Jr.

# The Church in the Postmodern World

John E Phelan Jr.

# The Church in the Postmodern World

**Understanding the Role of the Body of Christ in the 21st Century**

CHRISTIAN • LITERATURE • CRUSADE
FORT WASHINGTON, PENNSYLVANIA 19034

*CHRISTIAN LITERATURE CRUSADE*
*U.S.A.*
P.O. Box 1449, Fort Washington, PA 19034

*GREAT BRITAIN*
51 The Dean, Alresford, Hants. SO24 9BJ

*AUSTRALIA*
P.O. Box 419M, Manunda, QLD 4879

*NEW ZEALAND*
10 MacArthur Street, Feilding

*ISBN 0-87508-479-6*



This printing 2000



*Printed in the United States of America*

# The Church in the Postmodern World

In their provocative book *Resident Aliens*, William Willimon and Stanley Hauerwas describe growing up in the South of the forties and fifties. "Our parents never worried about whether we would grow up Christian. The church was the only show in town. On Sundays the town closed down. One could not even buy a gallon of gas. There was a traffic jam on Sunday mornings at 9:45, when all went to their respective Sunday Schools. By overlooking much that was wrong in that world—it was a racially segregated world, remember—people saw a world that looked good and right. . . . Church, home and state formed a national consortium that worked together to instill 'Christian values.' People grew up Christian simply by being lucky enough to be born in places like Greenville, South Carolina, or Pleasant Grove, Texas."[1]

I am myself a child of that same South, growing up in Nashville, Tennessee, and I can bear witness to the accuracy of their account. In Nashville it wasn't a matter of whether you went to church, but which church you attended. "Where do you go to church?" was not an uncommon question even for kids to ask. This is not to say all churches or persuasions were considered equal. In my high school there were Baptist kids (usually the Southern variety) and Church of Christ kids. There were only a handful of Roman Catholics, since most of them attended private Catholic schools. And then there were the ecclesiastical bottom-feeders like myself, members of independent congregations sometimes bearing exotic names and possessing even more exotic theologies. We were the interested observers in the ongoing battle between the Baptists and the Church of Christ. It was not unusual to hear heated discussion in homeroom, not about the virtues of a professional or college athletic team or a rock band, but about *baptism*. The Baptists were, well, *baptist*. The Church of Christ believed in baptismal regeneration. They took being *the* Church of Christ very seriously. To this day an older Church of Christ building in downtown Nashville has a cornerstone that reads A.D. 33. At least in those days, in my town, they believed if you weren't baptized in the Church of Christ you were going to hell. This, of course, offended the Baptists no end. There were more than a few arguments and, if I remember correctly, at least one fistfight.

My sympathies were generally with the Baptists in these fights because, not being Church of Christ, I was, so far as that group was concerned, to be confined to hell along with the Baptists. But of course the Plymouth Brethren, my home communion, had their arguments with both the Baptists and the Church of Christ. Be that as it may, I was raised, as were Willimon and Hauerwas, in a world now as strange to my kids as a Hasidic Jewish village in medieval Poland. Although pockets of that world still remain, it has, for the most part, passed as surely as that village culture of eastern Europe. What happened to it? Why did it disappear? And why, in my opinion, is this in many ways a good thing?

Hauerwas and Willimon are very clear on the beginning of the end for this old paradigm in the South. They "date the shift sometime on a Sunday evening in 1963. Then, in Greenville, South Carolina, in defiance of the state's time-honored blue laws, the Fox Theater opened on Sunday. Seven of us—regular attenders of the Methodist Youth Fellowship at Buncombe Street Church—made a pact to enter the front door of the church, be seen, then quietly slip out of the back door and join John Wayne at the Fox. That evening has come to represent a watershed in the history of Christendom, South Carolina style. On that night, Greenville, South Carolina—the last pocket of resistance to secularity in the Western world—served notice that it would no longer be a prop for the church."[2]

## The Marriage and Divorce

Let us take a quick glance at history. For centuries after the conversion of Constantine, the borders of the state and the Church were the same. Mission involved the conquest of territory as well as the saving of souls. You won *Norway* for Christ, not just the Norwegians. This combination of Christian territory and Christian church is what we now call Christendom. Christendom, of course, had been in trouble for a long time by 1963. The idea that the Church and state shared the same goals and that the entire people of a given land was the same as the membership of the approved church in that land had been under attack for hundreds of years. The United States was founded upon the belief that the state should show no preference for or offer no hindrance to the free exercise of religion. Regardless of the current—and in my opinion, misguided—stance of some of their heirs in this matter, the earliest Baptists were staunch supporters of the separation of Church and state. They had suffered greatly under state-sponsored religion in Europe and were not eager to see the system replicated in the new land.

But old habits die hard. And the conviction that the state should help the Church do its job persisted in spite of political, philosophical, and legal arguments to the contrary. So in Nashville, Tennessee, Greenville, South Carolina, and virtually everywhere else in the South, the state made certain that there was nothing else to do on Sunday mornings (and evenings for that matter) by making sure that all the grocery stores, clothing stores, car dealers, and especially movie theaters were closed. There were no Little League games on Sunday. Even professional or college games were held either on Saturday or Sunday evenings. Restaurants were open, of course. People had to have somewhere to eat Sunday dinner!

All that is gone. You can buy anything you want virtually anytime you want in both Nashville and Greenville. And I doubt that the current crop of students at Cohn High School spend much time arguing about baptism. Even in the small-town South you are as likely to see a family doing yard work as heading out to church on a Sunday morning. That last bastion of American Christendom, the South, has been breached. And, for the most part, it fell without a serious fight. The battle had, of course, been lost in other places at other times in the rest of the country. You all have your own stories to tell. But with the fall of the "Christian South," the myth of America, the Christian nation, was dealt a fatal blow.

## The Myth

Let me hasten to say that appearances can be deceiving. I am not convinced that the South I grew up in was all that "Christian" in the first place. In addition to the aforementioned vicious racism, the kids I went to school with, even the ones who argued theology, were not noticeably holier or more Christlike than the ones my kids go to school with.

Perhaps they could quote a few more Bible verses and knew the verses to more hymns, but much of their "faith" was nominal, cultural. This is why it all disappeared so quickly. There were plenty of *adherents* in the South of my youth, but not so many *disciples*. But the communal norm said you went to church, you had a religion—preferably Christian and, in my community, even more preferably Protestant. It was once even thought in the South that advancement on the job and even the realization of a political career required the right religious connections. That, of course, is no longer true. President Bill Clinton is no longer helped in the South by being a Southern Baptist.

But now American Christendom is dead. The state will no longer help the Church do its job. Whatever cohesion existed between Church and state has been fully eroded. The culture no longer wears even a patina of piety. People no longer go to church because it is the thing to do or because people would talk about them if they didn't. Culturally we no longer even make a pretense of having a moral consensus. Pluralism, both cultural and religious, is the order of the day. In addition to world religions like Islam and Buddhism, a lurid infestation of semi-Gnostic, so-called New Age religions is now prominent on the American religious menu. The United States and Canada now constitute one of the world's largest mission fields. And what's worse, the state no longer seems to need us or even care that we exist.

In the face of this, some Christians have

panicked. They have rushed to try to restore the lost Constantinian agreement between the Church and the state, the Church and the culture. Nostalgic for the good old days, they argue that the United States, if not Canada, is and always has been a Christian nation and we must call it back to its religious and cultural roots, using the force of law, if necessary, to do so. Laying aside the issues of whether we were ever particularly Christian in any meaningful sense, this is like trying to put Humpty Dumpty back together again.

## The Cost

Furthermore, the Church must now recognize that the support of the state came at a very high price. That price was the Church's identity and mission. Scholars like Canadian theologian Douglas John Hall and American Loren Mead have argued that the cultural accommodation of the mainline churches cost them their moorings. Accepting a privileged status vis-à-vis the culture led to a loss of identity and mission, in part because they began to take their cues from the culture and not the gospel.

I would argue that the evangelical churches are not far behind, no matter how comparatively successful they seem today. All of us should remember that the strength of the mainline churches from the late forties through the late sixties was followed by a precipitous decline in the last decades of the century. Evangelical churches are now in the position to suffer the same fate, if they continue their pursuit of cultural acceptability and political power. The belief that the Church must present the gospel to the culture in a "culturally relevant" way, or that the Church must "meet the needs" of the culture, runs the risk of lessening the Church's commitment to historic Christianity by seeking the lowest common denominator. Acceptance of the pragmatic and utilitarian values of the culture leads inevitably to a loss of mission and vision.

I would argue that the best thing that could happen to the Church, evangelical or otherwise, would be for it to lose its illusions about the use of the state and cultural dominance to effect the will of God in Western culture. The Church, evangelical or otherwise, must learn to resist accommodation to that culture with all its might. The Church is not called on to convert America or Canada or any other nation, but to call men and women of every country and nationality to Christ and to form a discipleship community called "the Church" from every kindred, tribe, and tongue to be a light in a dark world.

There is a second price attached to the state's providing the Church with a spiritual monopoly. Not only did this cost the Church its mission, historically, as a price for its cooperation, but the state insisted on calling on the churches to help it keep its citizens in line. So far as the state was concerned, the churches were to encourage its citizens to support the *state's* goals, to promote *its* causes, and, of course, to cheerfully *pay* for all of them. It called upon the

Church to encourage its young men (and now its young women) to fight and die in its wars, regardless of the worthiness of the cause or the character of the enemy. It expected deference to its leaders and approval of its national goals. It expected the Church, in short, to make sure its members were loyal to the state and its ideology. As long as the Church did all this, the state was little concerned about its theology or ritual. The Church was just one more supportive institution the state could call upon to realize its secular goals.

As a result of all this, members of churches have not always been willing or able to distinguish their responsibilities to God from their responsibilities to the state. Among Protestants, Luther's two-kingdom theology promoted the right of the state to require submission to the political authorities in realms of particular state concern. Some think this unfortunate doctrine was at least partially responsible for the susceptibility of many ordinary Germans to Adolph Hitler's arrogant guile. But in response to Hitler, members of this church also produced one of the most stirring documents of the twentieth century, the Barmen Declaration. This document clearly placed limits on the rule of the state. It declared in part: "We repudiate the false teaching that there are areas of our life in which we belong not to Jesus Christ but another lord, areas in which we do not need justification and sanctification through Him." It continues: "We repudiate the false teaching that the Church can turn over the form of her message and ordinances at will or according to some dominant ideological and political convictions." The Barmen Declaration insisted there were areas of the Church's life that were off-limits to the state.

Nevertheless, the lure of state power, of cultural acceptance, has always been seductive to the Church. Constantinianism linked the success and growth of the Church with the success and growth of the state. It made the expansion of the borders of the state the same as the expansion of the influence of the Church. This was ultimately ruinous for the Church. The day came when the state and the culture no longer really needed the Church. Where once the state had needed the Church to keep its citizens in line, it now had material success, money, and power to offer them. The fear of not getting or of losing these things was a much better inducement to support the goals of the state than the fear of the Church or God had been. This very fear is now used quite freely by the culture against the Church itself!

Western Evangelicals have been caught betwixt and between in this matter. Historically conservative in the political realm (at least in the United States), they have found themselves in recent years in the uncomfortable position of criticizing the state for various abuses of its power. However, the response of many Evangelicals has not been to radically question a Christian's identification with state and cultural power, but to attempt to set things right in Washington or Ottawa. This has also resulted in a blurring of the Church's vision and a loss of its sense of mission. It is too painful to realize we are no longer needed. It is too painful to accept our marginalization, so we attempt to recapture lost ground. But I would suggest there are advantages to our current status.

According to Douglas John Hall, as a result of the collapse of Constantinianism and the state's finding other means to control its citizens, the Church has been exiled.[3] Western Christians are now like the Jews who were driven from Jerusalem. We find ourselves in Babylon. The Babylonians don't care if we keep kosher or circumcise our children. They don't care if we follow the laws of God and remember the Passover. It is a matter of supreme indifference to them. We can do all these things as long as they don't get in the way of the Babylonians' goals. And if the Babylonians can win us over or use us to help them to reach those goals, it is so much the better for them. So how do we preserve our sacred identity in a secular land? How are we to be Christians in a no-longer-is-and-perhaps-never-was Christian America or Canada?

## Another Myth

Our problem is that we have so long been linked with our culture that we have confused its ways with the ways of the gospel. We must begin the hard work of disentangling ourselves from the culture and its goals. This will not be easy. Some of the culture's assumptions are virtually second nature to the Church. For example, one of the ways our culture continues to seduce us is through the "myth of progress." According to the "myth of progress," things are getting better and better all the time. Technology is solving all our problems, and the future is looking brighter all the time. This myth is a particularly North American one. It was born in the hopeful and bold time of the late nineteenth century. It is hard to say whether this myth was given strength by the advent of Darwinism or vice versa. Suffice it to say, the notion that human beings were the pinnacle of a long process of improvement was appealing. The great liberal churches of the late nineteenth and early twentieth centuries were convinced this would be "the Christian century." The Christian faith would sweep around the world and God's will would take hold everywhere. "Mission" was to conquer the world for Christ, taking new territory and bringing in the kingdom of God. The sweep of the kingdom was as inevitable as the evolutionary process, as certain as technological progress. In light of bitter world wars, brutal holocausts, and ecological disasters, this can only be seen as ironic. And yet, in spite of the horrors of the twentieth century, this myth remains alive and well. It is like a deadly virus we can't get out of our system. I believe it is particularly troublesome nowadays for Evangelicals. It is simply part and parcel of our American pragmatism.

Some Evangelicals, ironically, were originally suspicious of this myth. Their eschatology, if nothing else, suggested that the world was more likely to get worse than better. In fact, some circles welcomed things getting worse because it was a sign of the coming of the end. But in the United States, at least, this theological pessimism has clashed with a cultural optimism. Sometimes, in fact, the most theologically pessimistic have been among the most culturally optimistic. And yet, as a culture, in spite of everything that has happened, we continue to believe that if we just find the right technology, pass the right laws, elect the right people, things will turn out just fine. We remain hopeful in the face of all the negative evidence. Hall calls this "cheap hope," a parallel to Bonhoeffer's "cheap grace." He writes: "As North American Christians whose faith is tainted by ideological optimism, we are trying to answer all our problems without exposing ourselves to them as *real problems*." This leads us to shallow "quick fixes" that either "complicate the problems further, or postpone more catastrophic encounters with them to the generations that will follow ours." Our optimism, he argues, "is defensive, and what it seeks to defend from is truth." In a striking phrase he says, "Credulity is the deadly enemy of faith."[4]

For many this means a refusal to acknowledge the suffering of the world outside the borders of our communities or our country. Or if the suffering is acknowledged, it is assumed to be deserved. Such refusal to acknowledge suffering and injustice may involve mockery of the pain felt by our female colleagues when they are marginalized, irritation with the demands of our African-American brothers and sisters, and sheer ignorance of the issues faced by our various immigrant communities. Comfortable and secure in the middle class, we look to government and the organized church to protect what we have. Such complaints, such flies in the ointment, only threaten our equilibrium and must be ignored.

We hope the stock market improves our mutual funds and that too much immigration doesn't threaten the quality of our lives. We live in mortal, if unacknowledged, terror that something bad will happen to the economy and endanger our comfortable retirement, and we will countenance any absurdity to make sure it stays strong. We hope working-class wages won't go up too much and spur inflation. We sadly say that downsizing is just the way business has to be done today. We are sometimes more convinced of the truth of our economic theories than of our Christian theologies. I actually heard sober, intelligent economists recommending recently that a way to help the Japanese out of their economic crisis was to get them to learn how to consume more and not save so much! Maybe they need a few conspicuous American consumers as the new cultural missionaries to show them how to get into some serious debt!

We simply don't want to believe that we can consume too much or spend too much or grow too rich or too big. We expect that we should be able to climb the career ladder all the way to the top, and are outraged if anyone suggests there are or should be limits. As Hall puts it, "Few citizens of our nations are able to entertain the thought that there may be something so wrong with our 'world' that its righting would require of us, individually and corporately, acute sacrifices and dramatically changed expectations."[5]

## The Implications

The foregoing is just one example of our subtle accommodation to the culture. Nevertheless, it has huge implications for our ministries. When this understanding of things infects pastors and churches, we begin to believe that our task is simply to reassure a worried middle class that everything is going to work out OK. We use our worship services, our preaching and teaching, to help them adapt to the insecurities of living with great wealth. We teach them how to live as Christians without really having to sacrifice a thing. We help them to have stronger marriages, better-behaved kids, and healthier bodies, but we don't seriously call them to carry the cross of Jesus. We sing and celebrate all year long, making sure nothing negative or uncomfortable mars the joy of our worship. We make sin mere dysfunction and offer therapy rather than repentance. We assure them that God wants them happy and that they aren't responsible for the suffering of the world. When we do this, we are offering them "cheap hope" just as surely as the German church of Bonhoeffer's day was offering the German middle class "cheap grace." Of course, there is plenty of cheap grace around too.

## We Must Hope in Christ Alone

Christian hope is not hope in the economy, or hope in the government, or hope in the stock market, or hope in the retirement account, or hope in technology or power. Christian hope is hope in Jesus Christ crucified, risen, and coming again. To speak with integrity to this culture, we must put aside "cheap hope" born of the Western ideology of optimism and place our hope in Jesus Christ alone. Jesus Christ is Lord even if the stock market crashes and the economy collapses. Jesus Christ is Lord if our government falls and our borders are threatened.

How can we be the Church in this world and not be in pain? How can we be the Church in this world and not suffer? How can we be the Church in such an affluent culture and not be uncomfortable? Read Jeremiah again. Read about his anguish at the sin of his people. Consider his moral outrage at the injustice of the wealthy. Many Evangelicals can whip up outrage at the sin of others; but I suspect that sometimes that outrage is a comfortable mask for moral superiority. If I denounce the sins of others, it must mean that I am holy, or at least not as bad as they are. I would be more convinced if they wept for those sins rather than gleefully denouncing the sinners. We should remember that Jesus wept when He predicted the destruction of Jerusalem. How many of us have wept over genuine injustice in the world? How many of us have, rather, simply grown numb to it?

## Acknowledge Our Spiritual Numbness

We suffer from this numbness to injustice, I believe, because we have a "theology of glory" rather than a "theology of the Cross." This theology of glory is a natural development of the ideology of optimism, of cheap hope. The theology of glory resonates with Easter Sunday, not Good Friday. The theology of glory prefers spiritual gifts to thorns in the flesh. The theology of glory would rather count the five thousand being fed than the handful of faithful left at the foot of the cross. The theology of glory gets all excited about growth, statistics, and success stories and ignores suffering and struggle. Arrogance, pride, and ambition are not sins to be repented of, for the theology of glory, but character traits to be sought.

## Choose the Way of the Cross

In face of a culture both secular and ecclesiastical that glorifies self-aggrandizement, Jesus' call to humble cross bearing, to dying to oneself, to putting others first, remains normative for His disciples. When James and John *sought* positions of power, *asked for* positions of power at the right hand and left hand of Jesus, He denounced them. You will remember that Jesus said, "You know that among the Gentiles those whom they recognize as their rulers lord it over them, and their great ones are tyrants over them. But not so among you: but whoever wishes to be great among you must be your servant and whoever wishes to be first among you must be slave of all. For the Son of Man came not to be served but to serve and to give

His life a ransom for many." You will remember that He also said, "Those who want to save their life will lose it, and those who lose their life for My sake, and for the sake of the gospel, will save it. For what will it profit them to gain the whole world and forfeit their life?"

We live in a political world, and we are political people. It is right that we struggle for clarity on issues of mission and vision and leadership. Not only are we political people, we are sinners. In our struggles and questions, we have all from time to time soiled our hands and engaged in activities we regret. Having said all this, I still must declare that there is something more than unseemly about a struggle for power in the Church of Jesus Christ. Such struggling reflects a theology of glory, an ideology of power, rather than a theology of the Cross, an ideology of "weakness." Paul was told, when he sought the power of God for healing, "My grace is sufficient for you, for power is made perfect in weakness," and said, "Whenever I am weak, then I am strong." If we are to be the community of disciples following the crucified Jesus, we must repudiate this theology of glory born of the myth of progress and take up the theology of the Cross. This means that we reject the seductive lies of hierarchy and power, manipulation and intrigue, and take up the moral suasion of love.

## The Prescription

I have heard and spoken many gloomy and apocalyptic words about the future of the Church if this or that happens or if this or that person is elected to such and such an office (either secular or ecclesiastical). But cheap pessimism is no more appropriate than cheap hope. The kingdom is still God's! I am reminded of words from Eugene Peterson after an hour's worth of gloomy conversation with a group of veteran Christians moaning about the sorry state of the world. "These kinds of conversations always seem to me so futile. All these people around the table were Christians, *veteran* Christians, each with at least forty or so faithful years of worship and responsible work behind them. And here's the thing that struck me in the middle of the conversation; not a word in the conversation indicated any awareness of what Christ is doing or has done. It was as if Christmas and Easter and Pentecost had never occurred."[6] To repeat what I said earlier, Christ is still on the throne and working out His purposes for His world. We must pray His prayer with confidence, "Thy kingdom come, Thy will be done."

The Church in exile must cut itself free from the host culture. It must beware of absorbing its values, its vision, its mission. The ideology of optimism, the "theology of glory," is only one thing we have taken from our culture. But it is a deadly and insidious disease that will destroy us unless we undergo the spiritual surgery necessary to cut it out. We suffer from this disease because we don't recognize it as a problem. For us, "glory," success, and progress are part of the worldview we are born to and grow with. They seem as natural as the rain or the sunshine.

We have not challenged these cultural assumptions sufficiently from the Word of God. We rail against trivialities and ignore monstrosities; we strain out gnats and swallow camels.

### *Learn to Think Spiritually*

How are we to fight our tendency to ape our culture? How are we to fight our conformity to its destructive values? First, if we are to be Christians who can address this culture with the gospel—not just a warmed-over version of what the culture assumes already—we must become a studying, thinking, and reflecting people. We must be people who are learning to "do theology." We must be learned enough, wise enough, competent enough to know what is going on around us and within us. To quote Douglas John Hall once more: "Our churches do not need managers, they need thinkers! They need people whose knowledge of the Scriptures, traditions, and contemporary Christian scholarship is more deeply developed than has been required of clergy in the past. They need teachers, resident theologians, teaching elders, rabbis: learned persons who can prevent the faith from being reduced to platitudes and ethical truisms and pious reflections of the regnant 'values.' They need persons who know the literary and artistic traditions of Western civilization well enough not to be duped by cheap art and who understand the technocratic society sufficiently to know that it must be resisted."[7]

In spite of our shallowness and susceptibility to

every warmed-over heresy that comes along, there are those who would reduce training for the ministry to the mere acquisition of skills and pragmatic capabilities. Again, with Hall, "There is already such a slide toward anti-intellectualism and religious *kitsch* . . . in [the] remaining representatives of classical Protestantism that the trend can only be altered with the greatest effort. Perhaps for the majority it *cannot* be altered. Nevertheless, the effort must be made, because the alternative is the further trivialization of the faith and, finally, its relegation to sheer religious froth. And that is a fate too melancholy to contemplate for a faith that could move the intellects of an Augustine, an Aquinas, a Calvin, a Simone Weil, and countless others."[8]

A thinking Church is a counter-cultural Church and does *not* give in to the mindless pragmatism of Western culture, but challenges it to great intellectual and spiritual depth. All this means that our churches must be places of biblical learning and theological integrity. In an era of biblical illiteracy and theological naïveté, we more than ever need churches and pastors willing to wrestle with the Scriptures, with the great theological thinkers both ancient and modern, and with the challenges of a culture gone mad.

### *Restore a Missionary Mentality*

Second, we must not only be thoughtful, articulate, biblically and theologically literate people, we must be mission-oriented people. In *The Once and Future Church* Loren Mead suggests that the Church of the future must return "to one of the features of the Apostolic Ages" and see "the front door of the church as a door into mission territory, and not just a door to the outside."[9]

In spite of what state and culture tell us, we still need the Church! We need discipleship communities formed for learning, mutual support, and mission. We need these communities *not to be* incestuous, closed fellowships, but winsome, inviting, and exciting places. We need them to be clear about their mission of gospel proclamation and gospel living. Liberated from the task of being chaplain to the culture, these churches can compassionately but firmly challenge the culture's absurdities and offer a Christian counter-culture that is neither easy nor simple, but rich with possibilities for new life.

What does it mean for the Constantinian era to be past? For Christendom to be virtually ended? According to Loren Mead, "It means that God who called the church out into the apostolic world two thousand years ago is again calling the church out, this time into a secularized world where its mission and life must be once again redefined."[10] Yes. Redefined, but not reinvented. The mission and life have always been the same: to represent the crucified and risen Christ. Only now we do it with no illusions about the culture we live in. We are very much like Paul in Ephesus or Peter in Antioch. We are set down in a pagan culture, which no longer knows nor cares about the One we worship and the hope and love we share. But we believe we have good news for the world. How will we survive in such an environment? With Mead, "In the final analysis, the issue is one of mission. How do we as Christians—whether mainline or sideline, liberal or conservative, connectional or free—find a community that forms and sustains us in an authentic faith and move out bearing that faith into the structures of our ambiguous society? How do we pass those forms of community on to the next generation?"[11]

We must avoid the quibbling, backbiting, posturing, and pettiness born of a theology of power and glory. If we are to be a mission-minded Church, we must give up our foolish strutting, our ambition for power, and acknowledge that we are now in exile. We need the firm words and strong love of brothers and sisters in the discipleship community to communicate the gospel and love faithfully. If we squander both our heritage and our future in our struggle for power, we are doubly damned.

## The Call

What then is the specific mission of the Church in this generation? How will we carry it out? What do we do now that the rules have changed? How do we proceed now that the Constantinian era is past and we are once again just one option among many in a pagan world? We have noted how our current era is much like that of the primitive Church. We are a small, disenfranchised group of believers set down in a disinterested, pagan world. Given who we are and what we believe, how do we follow the command of our Lord to "make disciples of every nation"?

In his controversial and provocative book *The Rise of Christianity*,[12] sociologist Rodney Stark investigates how Christianity succeeded in establishing itself in the Greco-Roman world. Humanly speaking, how did this tiny, obscure Jewish sect make it through the welter of cults, sects, philosophies, and religions to ultimately dominate the Western world?

Stark begins by describing his early research on why people convert from one religion to another. He asserts that people convert for a very simple reason: the new religion offers them a better way of life. In studies of religious conversion in this century Stark and his colleagues found that "new religious movements mainly draw their converts from the ranks of the religiously inactive and discontented, and those affiliated with the most accommodated [i.e., worldly] religious communities."[13] These people, they found, convert not because of theology or ideology, but because of personal attachments to members of the religious group in question. Stark concludes, "The basis for successful conversionist movements is growth through social networks, through a structure of direct and intimate interpersonal attachments." And religious groups fail if they "become closed or semiclosed networks . . . if they fail to keep forming and sustaining attachments to outsiders and thereby lose the capacity to grow."[14] Conversion, in other words, may be as much about open, receptive, caring communities as it is about clearly defined theology. The theology, however, *is* important, as we will see, because *it* makes those communities what they are.

## The Lesson

How did the primitive Church convert so many people? How can the Church of the twenty-first century be as successful? Stark offers some remarkable examples of the ways the primitive Church reached out and engaged the pagan culture in the first three centuries of the Christian era.

First of all, according to the earliest and most important Christian historians, the Church's response to epidemics was a critical factor in its growth. According to Stark, in the ancient world "the epidemics swamped the explanatory and comforting capacities of paganism and of Hellenic philosophy. Not only were Christians at the forefront of caring for those stricken by the plagues, but Christianity offered a much more satisfactory account of why these terrible times had fallen upon humanity, and it projected a hopeful, even enthusiastic portrait of the future."[15]

Stark describes graphically the terror of plagues in the ancient world. The crowded cities of the ancient Near East were perfect breeding grounds for disease. Antioch, for example, is estimated during the early days of the Church to have had 75,000 inhabitants per square mile, or 117 per acre. By comparison, Chicago has 21 inhabitants per acre, San Francisco 23, and New York City 37. Keep in mind that Chicago, San Francisco, and New York contain this density within thousands of multi-story buildings, whereas in the ancient world most buildings had only one story, or three to five stories at the most. Stark reminds us, furthermore, that "modern New Yorkers do not share their space with livestock, nor are their streets fouled by horse and oxen traffic." He concludes, "Given limited water and means of sanitation, and the incredible density of humans and animals, most people in Greco-Roman cities must have lived in filth beyond our imagining."[16] No wonder epidemics and plagues frequently devastated the cities.

Christians became known for their compassionate care of the sick and dying during these plagues. Whereas the pagans who could fled the cities, the Christians remained and cared for the sick, often at the cost of their own lives. The pagan emperor Julian was clearly annoyed about this. He complained, in a letter, of the Christian "benevolence toward strangers and care for the graves of the dead." "The impious Galileans," he writes, "support not only their poor, but ours as well."[17] Stark argues that it was this compassionate presence with the suffering and dying that led in part to the growth of Christianity between the first and fourth centuries. On a practical level, since the most basic nursing care—providing food and water for those too weak to care for themselves—

greatly increased a sick person's chance for survival, it is likely that more Christians survived these plagues than pagans did. Second, when Christians cared for and saved the lives of pagans, they did so out of love and the conviction that their God promised a resurrection life. Not surprisingly, the pagans thus cared for were often converted to the faith of those who had bravely shown them compassion. The Church also provided a new social network for those who had lost family and friends to such plagues. This again made their conversion to Christianity natural. Christians' theology made sense because of their loving action on behalf of those who suffered.

This was not the only factor that led to the conversion of the Greco-Roman world. Many scholars have noted that, early on, Christianity was particularly appealing to women. Why was this? Men greatly outnumbered women in the Roman world. Scholarly work on population in the ancient world suggests that in Rome there were 131 males per 100 women, and 140 men per 100 women in Italy, Asia Minor, and North Africa.[18] Why were these figures so out of line? Historians suggest there were several factors. Consider the famous letter of Hilarion to his pregnant wife, Alis, from the early first century A.D.: "I beg you to take good care of our baby son, and as soon as I receive payment I shall send it up to you. If you are delivered of a child before I come home, if it is a boy, keep it; if a girl, discard it." In reliefs of Roman families one often sees more than one son, but never more than one daughter. It was common practice in the Greco-Roman world for excess daughters to be exposed and killed. Small wonder that men outnumbered women in the ancient world.

But there were other reasons. Abortion was frequent in the Greco-Roman world and was as deadly to the women as to their unborn fetuses. The description of abortion methods used in the ancient world is too gruesome to share here. If women did not die of the procedures immediately, they would often succumb to a postoperative infection. In the Roman world husbands had the right to order their wives to undergo such a procedure, as well as to expose an infant daughter. A female in the ancient world, then, was at risk not only at the time of her birth but throughout her life.[19]

Christians and Jews were opposed to both infanticide and abortion. It is not surprising, then, that women, so threatened by both, found such a faith congenial. Their very lives as well as the lives of their daughters were at stake! But there was another issue. Because of this shortage of women, girls were married at very young age in the ancient world. According to Stark, "typically, Athenian females were married at puberty and often before." Plutarch reported that Romans "gave their girls in marriage when they were twelve years old or even younger." Dio Cassius, a Greek writer, agrees: "Girls are considered . . . to have reached marriageable age on completion of their twelfth year."[20] According to evidence of inscriptions, Christian girls married much later. Stark reports: "Nearly half (44 percent) of the pagans had married by age 14 compared with 20 percent of the Christians. In contrast, nearly half (48 percent) of the Christian females had not wed before age 18, compared with a third (37 percent) of the pagans."[21] Christian women were not so often forced into an early marriage as their pagan sisters. This was also appealing to women in the Greco-Roman world.

When you add to this the relative status of women in the Church in comparison with those in pagan society, it is easy to see why women were drawn to Christianity. This resulted not only in more women who were Christians, but greater fertility among Christians. Opposition to infanticide and abortion meant that more babies were born. More Christian women meant potential marriages between Christians and pagans. The result of this was what are called "secondary conversions": pagan men who married Christians were often drawn to the faith themselves. Although some church leaders discouraged this practice, others actually encouraged it, citing such conversions.

A final reason for the many conversions in the ancient world lay in the fact that the Christian movement was an *urban* movement. And life in the cities was lived for the most part out-of-doors. The places people lived were too small and cramped to do anything but store goods and perhaps sleep. In those ancient cities you rubbed elbows with your neighbors constantly. You knew them intimately. You could hide very little. Discussions of the everyday matters of life were common. The hope Christians had found in Jesus Christ was seen in the compassion they showed for the suffering and dying, the new way they treated their women and slaves, and the pattern of honesty and integrity in their lives.

Stark sums it up this way: "To cities filled with the homeless and impoverished, Christianity offered charity as well as hope. To cities filled with newcomers and strangers, Christianity offered an immediate basis for attachments. To cities filled with orphans and widows, Christianity provided a new and expanded sense of family. To cities torn by violent ethnic strife, Christianity offered a new basis for solidarity. And to cities faced with epidemics, fire, and earthquakes, Christianity offered effective nursing services." He concludes, "No wonder the early Christian missionaries were so warmly received in [Antioch]. For what they brought was not simply an urban movement, but a new culture capable of making life in Greco-Roman cities more tolerable."[22]

We see, then, that Christianity grew by providing new ways of engaging some of the most pressing problems of life in the ancient world, problems the pagan world was failing to address. Their love of Christ and their hope for eternal life enabled them to face the epidemics with courage and optimism. Their conviction that "in Christ there is no male nor female" enabled them to afford women a new place in a formally closed society. Their reverence for all human life saved the lives of countless young women. Their work in the cities made life more livable. *Their theology, their beliefs, made their lives better, healthier, and more compassionate than those of their neighbors. Being a Christian was simply a better way to live!* According to the evidence provided by Stark, converts tend to be attracted to the way of life offered by the community and then, only secondarily, to its theology. Its theology, of course, was the *basis* for its way of life.

## The Challenge

What does all this have to do with today's Christianity and its future? Nearly everything! How are we going to leave the safe confines of our churches and reach this big, bad, postmodern world with the gospel? In the same way the ancient Church did. We need to show the world that the Christian life—following Jesus Christ—is the best, healthiest, most rewarding way to live. Having said this, I would hasten to say that we must beware of simply identifying this healthy and rewarding way of life with a typical middle-class American lifestyle. We are not talking here about a Christianized version of the American dream. That way of life has produced the hollowness, blandness, and shallowness that is now pervasive in our churches, schools, and neighborhoods.

Nevertheless, we must say that being a Christian is not just true, it is *good*. Unfortunately, we Christians have often given the world the impression that being a follower of Jesus is a long experience of misery and sacrifice. We have given the world the impression that we are an angry, unpleasant people who don't much like anyone. We are often seen as severe, cranky, out of touch. In *What's So Amazing about Grace?* Philip Yancey tells of asking people on planes what they think of when they hear the words *evangelical Christian*. "In reply mostly I hear political descriptions of strident pro-life activists, or gay-rights opponents, or proposals for censoring the Internet. I hear reference to the Moral Majority, an organization disbanded years ago. Not once—*not once*—have I heard a description redolent of grace. Apparently that is not the aroma Christians give off in the world."[23]

This is the aroma the Christian can and should give off. This is the way we can show a skeptical world that following Jesus is not an experience of miserable law-keeping isolation, but a joyful, familial celebration of a good and generous God. In Galatians Paul chides the church for falling back into the patterns of legalism from which Christ had rescued them. He compares them to children who have been under tutors and nannies. After they grow up and become adults, free to make their own decisions, why would they want to go back to the nanny again? In Christ they are grown-up men and women freed from the restraints of their nanny. That old nanny wasn't bad. Quite the contrary. If she did her job well, the lessons she taught were part of the essential character of the persons they had become. But a mature adult does not need to return to the ABCs.

A mature adult does not need to be told when and how to do absolutely everything. A mature adult does not need to be told how to think about absolutely everything.

Paul clearly expected the Galatians—and clearly expects us—to grow up. But I am very much afraid that Christians on both the left and the right have been stuck in a spiritual adolescence. We have not quite freed ourselves from the old nanny, nor have we become the mature, Spirit-directed people Paul thought would emerge. We have been caught between childhood and maturity, sometimes acting all grown up and sometimes acting like little children, pouting and throwing our toys. The Christian community had the chance early on to live out the exciting, liberating grace of God; but time after time, having left the law's cage, it reacted in terror to the freedom of mature adulthood. It either retreated to the legalisms of childhood or engaged in adolescent acting out. I would suggest it is the tendency of the right to retreat fearfully into the legalisms of childhood and the tendency of the left to engage in adolescent experimentation and acting out. Remember: the truly mature believer, so far as Paul is concerned, is the one who has *internalized* the will of God—who has the Word *written on the heart*.

The Church today has the opportunity to offer to the world a grown-up faith, a faith that can handle ambiguity, a faith that can handle hard questions, a faith that can accept people even when they are wrong, a faith that permits disagreements and encourages discussion, a faith that is able to say "I'm sorry" and "I love you," a faith that looks out for the suffering and marginalized and shares with them the love of Jesus. A faith that is mature because the Word and will of God are internalized! We have an opportunity, I say. Or we can fall back into the safety of the old nanny, or perhaps engage in adolescent acting out, refusing to leave either childhood or adolescence. So let us take heed.

There are all kinds of people in families. There's conservative Uncle Bob, who lives in the suburbs and votes Republican. There's liberal cousin Lisa, who lives in a city co-op and works with the homeless. One brother is an Army officer, another a devoted pacifist. One brother-in-law is a law officer in favor of capital punishment. His wife pickets at the prison whenever a life is to be taken. These opinions are real, profoundly different, and in some senses not compatible. But you stay together because you are a family and have a common ancestry and common commitment. You stay together because you are grown-up people, not adolescents. Jesus, as you know, called His disciples from all sorts of backgrounds and persuasions. He expected them to stay together, whatever their differences; because, however serious those differences, they had Him in common. And they had His mission in common: a mission of God's generosity, grace, and longing. God *does* want lost people found—and lonely people, and broken people, and confused people, and angry people, and frustrated people. God wants *all sorts* of people found and restored to the family. Today's Christian has a chance to help find such people, if he can avoid insularity, squabbling, and childishness, of which we are all capable.

We must ask ourselves, what are the plagues, the epidemics, of this day? They could be physical, psychological, or even intellectual. Who are the suffering people we should reach out to when everyone else is fleeing the city? How do we love these people and show them a better way of life? We must ask ourselves, who are the "women" of our day? Who are the marginalized people we can stand up for in generous and compassionate ways? Some would say, rightly, that in some ways women are still being denied a place at the table or only grudgingly admitted to the feast. But there are many others who for one reason or another are isolated in our society. The Church must show it is different by giving the ignored access to the family. Finally, how do we keep ourselves open to and connected with such people? For those of us who live in the suburbs, where people make great efforts to *limit* access and involvement with other people, this is a particularly challenging question. But we must answer it. And personally.

Finally, what Stark says about the need and opportunities of the city is as true today as it was then. The city is full of the marginalized, hurting, lonely, and maimed. A continuing revival of city ministries is crucial to the 21st century Church.

Recent statistics have suggested that, in reality, only about 20 percent of Americans are in church on a given Sunday morning. This means we have a huge challenge and an incredible opportunity. But we also need new strategies and greater compassion if we are to reach our culture as the ancient Church did its culture. May we find both.

O God, revive your Church. O my Lord, revive even me!

*John E. Phelan Jr. is president and dean of Chicago's North Park Theological Seminary. He has also served as a pastor and as the executive director of Covenant Publications in the Evangelical Covenant Church.*

## Notes

1. William Willimon and Stanley Hauerwas, *Resident Aliens* (Nashville Tenn.: Abingdon Press, 1989), 15–16.
2. Ibid., 16.
3. Douglas John Hall, *Confessing the Faith* (Minneapolis, Minn.: Fortress Press, 1996), xi.
4. Ibid., 466.
5. Ibid.
6. Eugene Peterson, *The Wisdom of Each Other* (Grand Rapids, Mich.: Zondervan, 1998), 70.
7. Hall, 195.
8. Ibid., 196.
9. Loren Mead, *The Once and Future Church* (Washington, D.C.: The Alban Institute, 1991), 25.
10. Ibid., 43.
11. Ibid., 92.
12. Rodney Stark, *The Rise of Christianity* (Princeton, N.J.: Princeton University Press, 1996).
13. Ibid., 19.
14. Ibid., 20.
15. Ibid., 74.
16. Ibid., 153.
17. Ibid., 84.
18. Ibid., 10.
19. Ibid., 120–121.
20. Ibid., 105.
21. Ibid., 106.
22. Ibid., 161–162.
23. Philip Yancey, *What's So Amazing about Grace?* (Grand Rapids, Mich.: Zondervan, 1997), 230.